Property-Emall Handbook

Partnership Acquisition to Operation

A guide to successful ownership and operations

By:

Rick Lundberg

Property-Email Handbook

Text – Copyright © 2018 Richard George Lundberg

Cover – Copyright © 2018 Richard George Lundberg

All Rights Reserved

Printed in the United States of America

Millennium Press

ISBN: 978-1719060967

Dedication

This business handbook is dedicated to all of those who have inspired and supported me through all of my business startups in the past and in the future.

Parents, John and Doris Lundberg

Grandparents, Andrew and Alma Lundberg

Grandparents, Willet and Bertha Roberts

Doctor George Ruggles

Judge A. C. Brown

Reverend Frank Johnson

Mayor Jerry Norene

Teacher Jay B. Johnson

US Army Captain Randall P Bartley

Engineer Harold P Bakke

And most importantly

My Loving and Wonderful Wife,

Marilyn Elaine Lundberg

Mission Statement

To provide ordinary people with an opportunity to build a business of their own, one that they create and nurture through a vision they have of their future. And to provide consumers with FREE access to search for virtually anything related to Real Estate.

Preface

Have you ever wondered why so many Companies charge hundreds of thousands of dollars for a Franchise?

It is because they have so few opportunities for a Franchise sale, and many Franchises come with a lot of risk, a lot of operational costs, and long-term hands on commitment from the Franchisee.

Those companies require their Franchisees to invest a lifetime of full-time management, education and involvement for a single Franchise. They have so many policies and rules, that a Franchisee would need to have an attorney on retainer to handle even the smallest of matters between the Franchisee and the Company.

Property-Emall does not sell franchises, we simply offer our **Marketing Associates** a chance for semi-retirement in a few years, no matter what age they are.

Marketing Associates may not have to hire ANY employees, if they don't want to.

Any Marketing Associate can very easily turn a single Marketing Territory which consists of five Zipcodes or Postal Codes, into a very comfortable middle-class family income in one or two years.

They can do it alone, or with a few partners, who can also acquire their own Marketing Territories.

There is no initial investment, except for an application fee to cover the cost of background and credit checks. The skills required are minimal. And the financial return is unlimited.

Executive Backgrounds

Founder and CEO:

Richard (Rick) Lundberg, has decades of Small Business experience. Since 1955, he has founded, or co-founded, over 40 small businesses, most with the help of his wife, or minority share partners. Some of which were sold, and many of which are still operating.

I was born in Minnesota, and lived the first 50 years of my life, in the Land of 10,000 Lakes.

My wife, Marilyn and I, moved to Texas as soon as we realized, that people in San Antonio, rarely see snow, and they don't pay State Income Taxes. That was in 1998.

Together, we have 4 children, one daughter and three sons. Together, the four of them have 11 children, five daughters and six sons. And right now, those eleven have one daughter, and two sons.

Education:

Forest Lake High School – graduated – 1965

Moorhead State College – English and Math majors – 1965 to 1966

Manhattan State University – Auto Body Repair Skills Certificate – 1970

Veteran's Administration OJT – Auto Body Journeyman Certificate – 1971

Anoka Technical College – Associate Degree in Construction Technology – 1972 to 1974

University of Minnesota School of Engineering – 1974 to 1975

Hennepin County Vo-Tech – Plumbing Inspector License - 1979

Dakota Technical College – Small Business Management – 1988

Hennepin County Vo-Tech – Small Business Management – 1989

San Antonio Board of Realtors – Texas Real Estate Salesperson License – 1999

San Antonio Board of Realtors – Texas GRI Designation - 2000

Minnesota License Board – Minnesota Real Estate License – 2002

Kaplan University – Texas Real Estate Broker License - 2003

California License Board – California Real Estate License – 2004

Various venues of Education – Business Management, Asset Protection, IRS Code, and Real Estate Continuing Education – 2001 to Present

Employment History:

St Paul Pioneer Press and Dispatch - Home Delivery – 1957 to 1960

Various part-time jobs – 1958 to 1964

Forest Lake Memorial Hospital – Janitor – Summer of 1964

Forest Lake Manufacturing – Piece work – Fall of 1964

Abrahamson's Nursery – Sales and Labor – Spring and Summer of 1965

Erickson's Gas Station – Attendant – Spring of 1966

Whirlpool Corporation – Assembly Line and Group Leader – 1966 to 1968

Forest Lake Shell Station – Attendant and Night Manager – 1966 to 1968

US Army – Pvt To SGT Infantry Rifleman – Jan 1968 to Mar 1970

US Army – SP5, Company Clerk – Mar 1970 to Sep 1970

Whirlpool Corporation – Night Foreman – Freezer Metal Finishing Group – Fall of 1970

Christiansen Chevrolet – Apprentice Body Mechanic – Winter and Spring of 1971

Pelican Valley Motors – Journeyman and Lead Body Mechanic – Summer of 1971 to Fall of 1972

Brooklyn Park Bowl – Night shift manger – Fall of 1972, Winter and Spring of 1973

Coon Rapids Metal Works – Welder – Summer of 1973

Elk River School District – Night Shift Janitor – Fall of 1973, Winter and Spring of 1974

BKBM Consulting Engineers – Drafting Technician – 1974 to 1977

BKBM Consulting Engineers – Project Manager – 1977 to 1982

Small Business Ownership & Management – SELF EMPLOYED – 1980 to Present

I am an Ordained Minister, a US Army Veteran, a Husband, a Father, a Grandfather, a Great-Grandfather, a Brother, an Uncle, the Oldest Lundberg in 4 Generations, a Caregiver, a Real Estate Broker, an Author, and an Entrepreneur.

Partner

Dixie Lyon

Dixie is a retired Lt Colonel, United States Air Force. She served as a Registered Nurse, and spent the last few years of active duty working directly for the Surgeon General in Washington DC.

After a short interval, she obtained her Real Estate License as an Agent with Keller Williams Realty. She started acquiring investment properties and has entered into three real estate partnerships with the Founder, Rick Lundberg.

She obtained her Real Estate Broker license, and is currently a Regional Director with Fathom Realty.

She has two children. A son who is an attorney in New York. And a daughter who is a Special Ops Trauma Doctor serving with the Elite Medical Group in the United States Airforce.

Partner and Website and Technology Director

Jason Roberts

Jason is the Founder and CEO of Jason Roberts & Associates, Inc. located in San Antonio, Texas. It is a creative services firm that is dedicated to helping others effectively communicate to their marketplace. The four primary pillars in the communication arts that are the foundation for this firm are: Graphic Design (print & electronic media), web site design & development.

Jason Roberts & Associates were also the original web design firm who helped to created this business website in 1999.

Future Partners and Officers offering exceptional talent will be announced in the future.

Company Description

Property-EMall, LLC is a Texas Limited Liability Company, which will be referred to elsewhere in this document as **"Corporate"**, is physically located on my small farm, in the Texas Hill Country, north of San Antonio. It is a web-based business, using www.propertyemall.com, to provide a marketing place for Real Estate Listings, and a database of suppliers and vendors. Almost every professional and skilled trades involved in the sale, the construction, and the maintenance of all forms of Real Estate will have a platform to advertise their business on **OUR** website.

In the Summary you will find an image of the old, currently being re-built, Mall Directory. The home page, and subsequent pages are in redesign. To get a snapshot peek at the original website, go to: https://web.archive.org/web/20000901090621/http://www.property-emall.com:80/index.html

This is a VIRTUAL mall, no machines, no bricks, no mortar.

Eight Corporate Partners will each own 5% of all shares, and upon acceptance by corporate will be able to select and acquire a Marketing Territory of their choosing.

Marketing Associate opportunities will give an Associate, exclusive rights to any sales in an area the size of FIVE Zipcodes or Postal Codes.

Any of the original partners, if they wish, in the future may sell their shares to another party, with majority approval of all other partners.

Market Research

I first, thoroughly studied this market in 1999. At that time, www.propertyemall.com, was the only web based real estate site to have international listings, with a retail store for resources and supplies, and a platform for which vendors and suppliers could advertise their businesses.

We weren't the only ones to realize that fact. About two months after we went live in 2000, a group of 5 investors from Tennessee offered me $5,000,000 for the business. I turned down the offer, because first, I didn't really need the money at that time, and second because the ten-year plan that I had written back then, had projected sales revenues in excess of $10,000,000 annually after 10 years. I didn't want a long-term plan, turn into short-term plan, and have to re-invest in another plan, for the long-term.

I didn't have the right plan for the growth I needed, and no partners to help me. We were live for 4 years, not quite breaking even, and still hadn't recovered any of my original investment. I took it offline, and waited patiently for the right plan, and the right time for this business.

That time is NOW!

The **good news** is, the market and economy have recently gotten better. The number of real estate listings is growing every day. The number of For Sale by Owner (FSBO) owners trying to sell their homes is growing every day. The percentage of homeowners who can actually perform simple repairs or maintenance on their homes is rapidly declining. And we won't be offering any services requiring a Real Estate License.

That was another obstacle I had to deal with before, as I was subject to every Multiple Listing Service (MLS) and Real Estate Commission's rules and regulations wherever I listed a property.

My recent searches of FSBO sites, reveal that they still only serve the FSBO. They provide inexpensive marketing tools, flat fee MLS, and links to bank foreclosures and Housing and Urban Development (HUD) sites. A few sites have links to a Mortgage Lender.

Websites providing lists of contractors and other services, such as Angie's List, HomeAdvisors, and Thumbtack, do not have real estate listings. They also charge their service providers a substantial referral fee, and some charge an additional fee on completed contracts.

FYI – Angie's List was founded in **1995** by Angie Hicks, in a small neighborhood in Ohio, where she went door to door to sign up consumers and service providers.

She did not have a profitable year until 2015.

She merged her company with HomeAdvisor in 2016. The combined parent company (ANGI Home Services) grossed over $7.6 Billion in revenues for 2017.

After all these years, NO ONE else is providing property owners with a one stop, one shopping experience, like they will find at www.propertyemall.com!

Products and Services

The home page of the www.propertyemall.com is designed to represent a Mall Directory. Each store on the Home page, will have a hotspot, when clicked on, will take the viewer to a page to select the Zipcode, for service providers who can provide the skill sets they are desiring, at the mere CLICK of a button.

There will be a FSBO store with links to For Sale by Owner listings throughout the United States. A Real Estate Agent store with links to National Realtor Associations throughout the world, where Sellers and Buyers, both, can search for FREE, by State, City, Zipcode, or International Postal Code for real estate listings.

This is the yard sign that my wife, Marilyn created for Property-EMall in 1999.

We want to stay VIRTUAL! No Brick and Mortar, needed or necessary, for a while anyway!

Marketing/Sales Plan

The Marketing Plan is simple. It will be done through and by Corporate and Marketing Associates.

All Marketing Associates will be Independent Contractors, whether they are individuals or business entities.

As mentioned before, a marketing territory will be FIVE contiguous or nearly contiguous Zipcodes.

If you have a spouse, a friend, or a partner who wants to become a Marketing Associate, they can get their own Territory, and any Service Provider that wants to jump over the border in either direction gets credited to the Marketing Associate who ends up with the Ad.

HOW MANY ZIPCODES ARE THERE IN THE UNITED STATES? MORE THAN 42,000!

The Marketing Associate will contact businesses, doing business, in his or her territory. The purpose is to secure an advertising agreement, which Corporate will provide. The business will pay Corporate a $10 monthly per Zipcode for a Standard Ad. Premium ads for $15 per month, and Platinum ads for $20 per month per Zipcode are available also. Yearly, or longer terms, will have discounts on rates negotiated with Corporate. The number of business listings for ANY of the trades or disciplines, will be limited to a maximum of 21 each for Standard Ads, per Zipcode. Premium and Platinum ads are unlimited. There are over 230 different categories, so roughly 4800 advertising spots per Zipcode.

The initial contact will be made by searching the internet for service providers who have an online presence already. After some research I have found that Yahoo has the most listings at this time. Marketing Associates will find that in the service provider category they are searching for across the 5 Zipcodes the number of current advertisers in each Zipcode will vary significantly.

The way I select my first call is easy.

Each new ad is placed in a First Come / First Listed basis.

Start by calling the lowest-ranking current ad and offering the highest-ranking advertising spot in any or all 5 of your Zipcodes.

The Advertising Agreement is month to month and they can cancel at any time. They won't though, as once they get a couple or a few referrals through us they will see the very affordable value in staying with us.

OH! By the way, each Zipcode will have its own website. That's right! For example, Your website will be www.propertyemall.com/12345 and so on through www.propertyemall.com?12349 .

The service provider enters in all of their information directly on our website. That information goes into our database, including the Zipcode which is automatically linked to the Marketing Associates Account, giving them the credit for that sale, regardless of where the lead came from. The Marketing Associate gets paid commission on that ad whether they had anything to do with it or not!

What comprises the Marketing Territory?

Using the Marketing Associates initial Zipcode as the center point, and surrounding it with FOUR adjacent or contiguous Zipcodes, will comprise a Marketing Territory. The strategy is, if for example, a Plumber has their business office in any one of the Zipcodes, they probably do work in all five Zipcodes. They may want to secure one of the advertising spots in all five Zipcodes.

The sales will break down like this:

For any advertising sales, the monthly fee will be $10 per month per Zipcode for a Standard Ad. The Standard Ad listing contains the Business Logo, Name of the business, and Website or URL link for consumers to get additional contact and information about the Advertiser.

For $15 per month per Zipcode, the Premium Ad listing contains the Business Logo, Name of the business, Website or URL link, plus a 50-character tag line, for example; "Proudly serving the area since 1989" or "Quality work on time and FREE estimates"

For $20 per month per Zipcode, the Platinum Ad listing contains the Business Logo, Name of the business, Website or URL link, Phone Number, and a 500-character brief description of the company.

The biggest difference is again "Who wants to be on top or as close to the top of the page as possible."

For all advertising sales, the Associate will be paid a commission of 50% for the first $20,000 worth of sales, and 70% thereafter for each Market Territory.

At some point in time, every State and US Territory, will have a Regional Director. In the case of California and Texas, they will each of 4 Regional Directors. Regional Directors will be appointed by Corporate, and, whose income will be based on personal marketing sales, and 1% of all Corporate profits, derived from all sales, in his or her state.

Financial projections

This is an opportunity, and a vehicle for ANYONE, who considers themselves one of ANY WORKING CLASS, to elevate their position, to any level they have ever dreamed of!

Here is where assumptions and very conservative estimates will come into play!

Let's start with the Marketing Associate, who has one territory consisting of 5 Zipcodes. Think of it as the original Zipcode, surrounded by neighboring Zipcodes to the North, East, West, and South. The chances are pretty good that service providers would want to expand their market area, and thus, their advertising.

The Marketing Associate is an Independent Contractor, having start-up costs of forming their own LLC, and some recording fees, which may be less than $1,000.

There are a lot of tax and asset protection advantages to running your business, as a business. If you do it as a sole proprietor you will be subject to Self Employment tax of 15% off the top of your Gross income. Then pay income tax on the Net income.

Now let's assume that the Associate is able to sell advertising spots at an average rate of 40 per month. That is only 10 per week, or 2 per day. Let us look at **a Group of Five**, where he or she consistently sells 40 spots per month.

Since this is residual income, each month ADDS one month's income on to the previous month.

40 spots X 5 Zipcodes = 200 sales X $10 = $2,000

Month	Gross Sales Income	Marketing Associate Commission
One	$2,000	$1,000
Two	$4,000	$2,000
Three	$6,000	$3,000
Four	$8,000	$4,000
Five	$10,000	$5,000
Six	$12,000	$6,000
Seven	$14,000	$7,000
Eight	$16,000	$8,000
Nine	$18,000	$9,000
Ten	$20,000	$12,500

Month 10 is the point where the commission split changes from 50% to 70%, after having reached the $10,000 limit to corporate for each of FIVE Zipcodes.

Eleven	$22,000	$13,900
Twelve	$24,000	$15,300
Thirteen	$26,000	$16,700
Fourteen	$28,000	$18,100
Fifteen	$30,000	$19,500
Sixteen	$32,000	$20,900
Seventeen	$34,000	$22,100
Eighteen	$36,000	$23,500
Nineteen	$38,000	$24,900
Twenty	$40,000	$26,300
Twenty-One	$42,000	$27,700
Twenty-Two	$44,000	$29,100
Twenty-Three	$46,000	$30,500
Twenty-Four	$48,000	$31,900
Twenty-Five	$50,000	$33,300

This Associate has only filled 1,000, approximately 20% of their available advertising spots for their Five Zipcode Group!

I believe that a Marketing Associate, could fill 70% of their available advertising spots without too much effort as the number of visitors to our site increases.

We will be aggressively marketing our business through all types of media. Driving consumers to our site using both real estate links and promoting our outstanding service providers.

Let's continue on …………………..

Twenty-Six	$52,000	$34,700
Twenty-Seven	$54,000	$36,100
Twenty-Eight	$56,000	$37,500
Twenty-Nine	$58,000	$38,900
Thirty	$60,000	$40,300
Thirty-One	$62,000	$41,700
Thirty-Two	$64,000	$43,100

Thirty-Three	$66,000	$44,500
Thirty-Four	$68,000	$45,900
Thirty-Five	$70,000	$47,100

In less than 3 years our Marketing Associates could be grossing $47,100 per MONTH, of RESIDUAL INCOME!

That is a whopping $565,200 per year of RESIDUAL INCOME!

With just over 42,000 Zipcodes in the United States there is an opportunity for 8400 Marketing Associates to become independently wealthy in a very short period of time.

When a Marketing Associate has reached a point where 50% of all available advertising spots have been filled, he or she could choose to just maintain their business, or continue to grow their business.

At any point in time they could have hired someone or could have taken on a partner to help them grow their business even faster.

They will have demonstrated that they have the skills to take their business to the next level.

A self-disciplined and motivated Business Owner / Entrepreneur will find a way to secure a legacy for themselves and their family by diversifying or expanding their businesses.

When Marketing Associates have reached the goal of filling 70% of available advertising spots for FIVE Zipcodes, they will qualify for an additional marketing territory.

Or pick a single Zipcode or Postal Code anywhere you like to vacation in, and then take that opportunity to conduct your Annual Business Meeting!

Check with your tax preparer to see how much of that trip you can deduct on your income tax.

Marketing Associates will receive their commission paid directly into their bank account, for their sales, no later than the 28th day of the following month.

AND IT WILL ONLY GET BETTER EVERY YEAR AFTER THAT, UNTIL WE FILL 42,000 ZIPCODES IN THE UNITED STATES!

GROSS INCOME for 42,000 Zipcodes at $14,400 net advertising fees to Corporate comes to: $604,800,000 residual income every MONTH!

I don't know how long it would take to get to that point, but since our Marketing Associates have no limits on what they can do over the years, someday we could be there!

You do the math to set your goals!

Remember, you start with FIVE, and build from there!

My advice – start with the Zipcode you live in or one close to you, then pick the four adjacent Zipcodes.

We have the opportunity to get it started!

Pass it on to our kids, and their kids!

THIS IS A LEGACY MAKER FOR ANYONE WHO GETS ON – BOARD!

Marketing Associate Applications

Individuals, Small Groups, or Business Entities may begin the application process by filling in an application from our website www.propertyemall.com. All applicants will be asked to supply information, along with an application fee of $100, per individual, to cover the costs of background and credit checks.

Once Corporate has reviewed the background and credit checks, and deemed that the applicant would be an asset, Corporate will send a confirmation form to the applicant.

Upon further review of the Application, and approval by Corporate, a copy of the Associate agreement will be given to the applicant for review and execution, along with confirmation of availability of desired Zipcodes.

Final acceptance by all parties, will occur when all documents have been signed by all parties.

FROM APPLICANT TO ASSOCIATE

THE BUSINESS MODEL

Looking back to the Business Plan, you will recall the business model for Corporate, which will also work for the Associate's Business Model.

If you founded your Marketing Associate Agreement as a Sole Proprietor, it is not too late to form a Limited Liability Company, or LLC, and inform Corporate of your new Business Entity. We can easily modify the Marketing Associate Agreement and the banking information.

There are a couple of ways to form an LLC. The first way is to find a local attorney who can assist you, which will cost you A LOT of money. The second way is to go online to any number of companies willing to assist you.

Just make sure you are getting the most protection from your LLC that the law allows. Not all clauses within the formation documents are the same everywhere.

See the book written by Rick Lundberg, entitled "2018 – The Year of the Entrepreneur". Available at amazon.com or Barnes & Noble, or go to www.ricklundberg.com to click on any or all of the books written by Rick or his wife Marilyn.

It explains in detail all of the different types of business entities, and why they each have their own pros and cons. If you have any questions, please consult with an attorney.

As your business grows you may want to expand and diversify your business, and further protect you and your family's assets from the IRS, and other predators.

The Business Plan also calls for ownership shares to be broken down between yourself and partners. The LLC suggests multiple partners in order to function properly.

The last thing you want to do is to take ANY income personally, thus avoiding the Self Employment Tax, which is currently 15% right off the top.

Your Franchise LLC should have a General Partner which owns a small fraction (say 5%) of the partnership shares. The General Partner, is the only partner liable for any debts, losses, or claims. And is only liable to the extent of the shares that it holds. In this case, 5%. The General Partner should also be you, or a Business Entity which ONLY YOU control.

The remaining partners are all Limited Partners!

The next partner is you. You should own 50%, if you are married, of the total shares. Your income from the LLC, comes to you (or your Living Trust) in the form of Dividends each month. If you are single, then 55%.

If you are married, then your spouse should own the next 5% of the shares. So, between yourself and your spouse, you now control 60% of the total shares.

The greatest control, still rests with you, as the General Partner, and as an individual representing yourself, or your Living Trust, controlling either 55% or 60% of the LLC.

The remaining 40% should be divided among 8 Limited Partners each owning 5% of the shares.

Now, you may not feel it necessary to have partners. That's fine! Just be sure that you are capable of soliciting the advertising, and managing your new business.

These partners are invaluable assets to your business. They need to trustworthy, reliable, and share your vision.

They may help fund your start-up costs, with their purchase of shares. You will encourage them to help secure the advertising contracts for the LLC for many reasons. One of which, is the almost immediate return on their investment in your Partnership, through monthly dividends. The second reason is, they will quickly see the benefits of starting their own LLC as well. This is an excellent opportunity for you to become one of their 5% partners, creating another stream of income for yourself.

Selling the Advertising

You will want to find vendors and contractors that already have an online presence.

Right now, the prime target would be current service providers on Yahoo. We don't want to take any potential leads away from our new clients. We simply want to give them an affordable alternative in addition to any other referral systems they are using.

WARNING! Do not call the service provider's phone number listed on the Angie's List, HomeAdvisor, or Thumbtack website. As that provider will be charged a referral fee on that call. He or she might not find that amusing!

Write down the contact information and go online to find the best way to contact them at no charge.

Next, start googling professions and services in your Marketing territory. For example: type in the search window – "painters in Zipcode 12345" and see how many come up. These are the next to contact in each category.

Corporate can forward you an Excel Spreadsheet with all of the categories already listed. Just send your request to admin@propertyemall.com .

I would recommend calling them directly first. Ask them if you can send them information on propertyemall.com and if the answer is yes, then send them a link to your website – www.propertyemall.com/12345.

Point out the fact that in the FSBO and Realtor stores in the mall, you have every property listing for sale, with hundreds, if not thousands of buyers and homeowners, visiting your site every week. Many of those visitors are looking for skilled contractors, and professionals to perform services on their properties, preparing them to sell, repair, or remodel their existing homes. The cost to advertise each month is $10 or more, depending on the contract they choose, per Zipcode. Once you start getting contractors on board it will be a lot easier to sell the remaining spots in each of the over 230 categories in YOUR mall.

We have a couple of cold call scripts that are also available if you are not an experienced salesperson.

You may want to knock on a few doors. Pass out business cards (available in our Store) or put on a luncheon meeting somewhere, and offer free food or snacks to attendees, where you can make a group presentation, and answer any questions they have.

Depending on your other activities and obligations, you might only be able to do this part-time at first, but once the money starts rolling in each month, selling advertising will soon prove itself to be very lucrative.

Corporate reserves the right to sell advertising in any Zipcode not under Marketing Territory protection and receive 100% of those advertising fees, until that Zipcode is assigned to a Marketing Associate, at which time the Associate will inherit those advertising contracts. There may be a fee added to the Agreement in those Zipcodes depending on the number of contracts already obtained by Corporate.

Remember, with around 4800 potential advertising spots in each Zipcode, if you sell them all, that is a minimum of $168,000 PER MONTH gross residual income for each Territory assigned to you.

And you basically only have to sell them ONCE for a lifetime of residual income.

You may have some attrition occasionally, requiring your attention to maintain a full house.

Corporate will have tracking in place to show each vendor how many click-thrus they get each month through your Website. It will be their obligation to convert click-thrus into sales and cash.

Recommended Financial Structure

Corporate Breakdown of all Gross Income will be as follows:

Foundations & Charitable Organizations:	10%
Marketing:	20%
Operating Expenses:	10%
Escrow for Taxes & Insurance:	30%
Shareholder Dividends:	30%

We recommend that successful Marketing Associates follow a similar plan:

Foundations & Charitable Organizations:	10%
Marketing and Operating Expenses:	20%
Escrow for Taxes, Insurance & Expansion:	30%
Shareholder Dividends:	40%

Other tips and guidelines

All of your commission revenue will go directly into the bank account linked to you or your LLC and the Federal Employer Identification Number (EIN) you entered on IRS Form W-9 in your application.

You should also have software for your accounting and tax preparation that can import information from your bank.

I have used Quickbooks and Turbo Tax, from Intuit for almost 20 years now, and I am currently the Tax Matters Partner, for over 20 business entities that I, or my wife own, or are the majority shareholders of.

Summary

Property-EMall LLC, has the best opportunity, right now, to explode onto a market that has been relatively stagnant for almost 20 years, and was non-existent before that.

Past regulations, taxation, and the economy have stifled growth. Small Businesses create a better future for all levels of society. Businesses who re-invest in their businesses, through innovation and generosity, will become recognized as cornerstones and leaders in their communities, and their industry.

There are businesses who provide some of the services which we will be providing. But, none are providing access to resources for the consumer, like we will.

Our marketing and advertising for Real Estate Sales by Owners, and National Real Estate Multiple Listing Services Worldwide, will be unparalleled.

Below is a poor snapshot, of a snapshot, of the Home Page, taken May 20, 2000 by Network Solutions, the Website Host.

They were not the Website Builder. I designed and directed the construction of the site using a local firm. That same firm has come on board to partner with us in creating and maintaining this new redesign which requires the latest technology now and in the future. I am pleased to have their commitment and expertise.

Look for yourself! On the internet, go to www.wayback.com, wayback machine, search for property-emall.com, then look at May 20, 2000. There are about a dozen pages you can look at.

If you want to see it NOW, simply go to

propertyemall.com

There wasn't anything like it then, and there isn't anything like it now!

The estimated sales projections, previously detailed, in this plan, are conservative. They are based on low, entry level fees, and what I believe to be, low sales. The advertising rates are very competitive. Much lower than our competitors. Once we load up FSBO listings, and Realtor listings, the traffic volume will rush through our website. Which will create a reason for trades and professions to **come to us**, wanting to be on our lists of vendors.

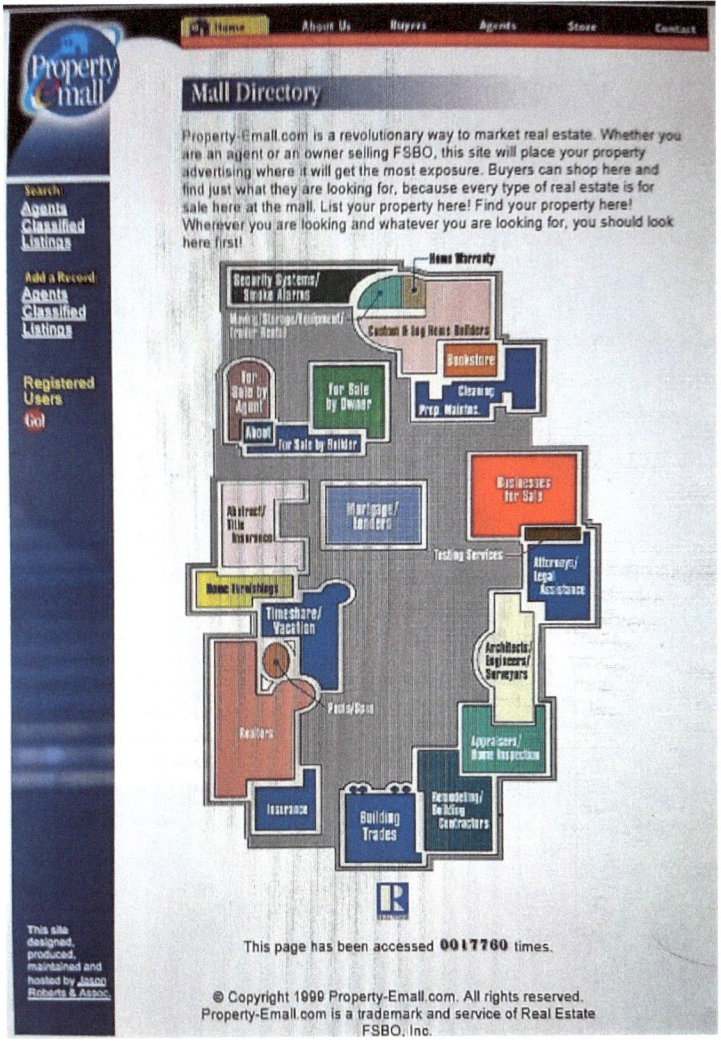

The website as was created in 1999.

The bottom line is this:

Good things can come in small packages!

I am seeking EIGHT original partners in Property-EMall LLC, willing to help this business grow. Partners can be individuals, groups, or business entities with a vision!

We will be up live around the start of 2019, and then we can start hiring Marketing Associates and sell advertising. You don't have to live in your chosen Zipcode, but it would be a good place to start for your first Franchise territory. Think outside the Box! Once we go live, prime Zipcodes will be the first to go.

Lastly, please contact me. It will be my pleasure to answer any questions you might have.

Sincerely and God Bless,

Rick Lundberg

rick@propertyemall.com

CORPORATE CONTACT INFORMATION

AT THIS PRINTING, January 2019

CEO: Rick Lundberg

Email: rick@propertyemall.com

Books by the Author:

Available Now:

"Golden Eggs" for Empty Nesters

2018 – The Year of the Entrepreneur

Property-EMall Handbook

The Evolution of Adam – Book I – The Child & The Boy

The Evolution of Adam – Book II – The Young Man

Upcoming Books:

The Evolution of Adam – Book III – The Soldier

The Evolution of Adam – Book IV – The Man

The Evolution of Adam – Book V – The Middle-Aged Man

The Evolution of Adam – Book VI – The New Man

The Evolution of Adam – Book VII – The Changed Man

The Evolution of Adam – Book VIII – The Obedient Man

The Evolution of Adam – Book IX – The Reflective Man

Books by the Author's Wife:

Available Now:

Identifying & Healing – Victory over Abuse Series Book I

God Your God – Victory over Abuse Series Book II

Contamination to Transformation – Victory over Abuse Series Book III

Jagger's Eyes

Upcoming Books:

To be Announced

www.ingramcontent.com/pod-product-compliance
Lightning Source LLC
Chambersburg PA
CBHW040239220526
45473CB00001B/305